1 MONTH OF
FREE
READING

at

www.ForgottenBooks.com

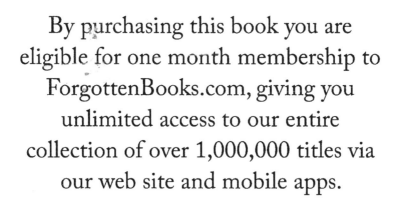

By purchasing this book you are eligible for one month membership to ForgottenBooks.com, giving you unlimited access to our entire collection of over 1,000,000 titles via our web site and mobile apps.

To claim your free month visit:

www.forgottenbooks.com/free858705

ISBN 978-0-483-19185-3
PIBN 10858705

AN

INTRODUCTORY TREATISE

ON

ELOCUTION;

WITH

PRINCIPLES AND ILLUSTRATIONS ARRANGED FOR
TEACHING AND PRACTICE.

BY

PROF. MARK BAILEY,

INSTRUCTOR OF ELOCUTION IN YALE COLLEGE.

NEW YORK ∴ CINCINNATI ∴ CHICAGO

AMERICAN BOOK COMPANY

Entered according to Act of Congress, in the year 1863, by

MARK BAILEY,

In the Clerk's Office of the District of Connecticut

Copyright, 1880 and 1908, by MARK BAILEY.

CONTENTS.

AN

INTRODUCTORY TREATISE

ON

ELOCUTION;

WITH PRINCIPLES AND ILLUSTRATIONS, ARRANGED FOR TEACHING
AND PRACTICE.

BY PROF. MARK BAILEY,

INSTRUCTOR OF ELOCUTION IN YALE COLLEGE.

PREFACE TO THE INTRODUCTION.

GOOD READING includes a mastery of the elements of language and elocution. *Articulation* and *pronunciation* must be
not only distinct and accurate, but expressive. This last excellence cannot be attained by merely enunciating meaningless
sounds and syllables. Too many such mechanical exercises
kill the instinctive use and recognition of expressive tones
which the child brings to school, and in the end completely
divorce his elocution from the spirit and sense to which it
should be inseparably wedded, and which alone can inspire
natural expression. The child feels and thinks before he
talks. Nature, in her teaching, begins with the idea, and in
her repeated efforts to express the idea more perfectly, perfects

the elementary parts of language and elocution. Let us enlist Nature into our service by following her teachings. Let even the earliest lesson in reading be enlivened by the aid of some idea familiar and interesting to the child. He knows the thing, the idea, "man," or "sun"; he has spoken the word a thousand times, and he is pleased to learn that the mysterious art of reading is only conscious talking, — that he is but analyzing, and sounding, and naming the unknown parts of a familiar whole. But especially with the advanced classes (which are expected to use the following work on elocution) would the author commend this practical method of improving the parts, with the immediate purpose of giving better expression to the whole, — of practising and perfecting the execution of the dead elements of elocution, in the life-giving light of inspiring ideas.

"There is in souls a sympathy with sounds."

This analogy in Nature between tones and sentiments is the central source from which the author has drawn the simple principles and hints which are given to aid teachers in their laudable efforts to cultivate in the school-room, and thus everywhere, a more natural and expressive elocution.

The art, embracing the expression of the whole range of human thoughts and feelings, from the earliest lispings of the child to the most impassioned and finished utterance of a Garrick or Siddons, covers too wide a field, and reaches too high a point in human culture, it is evident, to be all compressed into these few introductory pages; nor would the highest refinements of the art be practicable in the school-room if they could be here given. Yet such initial steps have been taken, and clearly marked out in the right direction towards the highest art, it is hoped, as will tempt many to go on farther in this interesting study of nature and art, till they see for themselves to what "rich ends" our "most poor matters point."

M. B.

PART I.

ELOCUTION is the VOCAL EXPRESSION of IDEAS with the *speaking* tones, as distinguished from the singing.

GOOD ELOCUTION, in reading or speaking, is the expression of ideas with their *appropriate* or *natural* speaking tones of the voice.

But how can we, intelligently, even *attempt* to give *correct vocal expression* to what is not first CLEARLY UNDERSTOOD and APPRECIATED?

Hence arises at the very outset, as a prerequisite to any possible excellence in elocution, the necessity of a THOROUGH ANALYSIS and STUDY of the *ideas* or the *thoughts* and *feelings* to be read.

Let, then, each lesson in reading begin with this *preparatory* work of "*Logical Analysis.*"

METHOD OF ANALYSIS.

In any *other* art, if we wish to *conceive* and *express* things *clearly*, we inquire, first, for the GENUS, or the GENERAL KIND; secondly, for the SPECIES, or the INDIVIDUALS, under that kind.

If, for example, we were asked to *paint* a group of animals or flowers, —

1. We should ascertain *what kind* of animals or flowers is meant — the horse, or the lion; the rose, or the lily.

2. We should determine the *peculiarities* of the *individuals*.

3. We should feel obliged to learn something of the *general colors* we are to paint with, their *various shades*, and how to blend these into *expressive* lights and shades. Then only should

we feel prepared to take the *first step successfully* in the art of painting.

Let us, in the kindred art of *elocution*, adopt the same *natural* method and order of inquiry.

Let us determine, —

1. The *general spirit* or *kind* of the piece to be read.
2. The *important individual ideas*.
3. The *relative* importance of the ideas.

1. We must determine the *kind* or general spirit, that we may know what general or *standard force*, and *time*, &c., of voice we should read with. There must be some *standard* to guide us, or we cannot tell *how much* emphasis to give to any idea. "Read the emphatic words *louder*," says the teacher. Louder than what? "Louder than the unemphatic words." But *how loud* are *they* — the unemphatic words? This question must be answered *first*, or we have no *standard* to go by; and the answer to this question is determined always by the *general spirit* of the piece. If *that* is unemotional, the standard force required is *moderate;* if bold, the standard force is *bold*, or *loud;* if subdued or pathetic, the standard force is *subdued*, or *soft*.

2. We must determine the *important individual ideas*, that we may know *what words* need *extra* force or emphasis.

3. We must determine the *relative* importance of these ideas, that we may know *how much* emphatic force we must give to each respectively, so as to bring out in our reading, clearly, the *exact* and *full meaning* of the author.

But it may be objected that this method of catching the spirit of the author, *first*, is too difficult for the school-room, because there are so many emotions not easily distinguished or remembered. Yet, since this *natural* order of inquiry, if it can be made *practicable*, will make all our after progress so much more intelligent and rapid, and since the chief charm of all the best pieces for expressive reading lies in the *emotional* part, let us see if we cannot sufficiently *simplify* these difficulties, by grouping nearly all the emotions into a *few representative classes,* which will be *definite* enough for all ordinary purposes in teaching elocution, and which can be *easily* recognized by any one who can distinguish joy from sorrow, or a mere matter-of-fact idea from impassioned sentiment.

As appropriate answers to our *first question* in analysis, let pupils become familiar with some such simple and comprehensive classes as the following : —

DIFFERENT KINDS OR CLASSES OF IDEAS.

1. ' *Unemotional,'* or *matter-of-fact* (whether didactic, narrative, or descriptive).

2. ' *Bold* ' (including the *very emphatic* passages in the first class, and all declamatory pieces).

3. ' *Animated,* or *joyous* ' (including all lively, happy, or beautiful ideas).

4. ' *Subdued,* or *pathetic* ' (including all gentle, tender, or sad ideas).

5. ' *Noble* ' (including all ideas that are great, grand, sublime, or heroic).

6. ' *Grave* ' (including the deep feelings of solemnity, reverence, &c.).

7. ' *Ludicrous,* or *sarcastic* ' (including jest, raillery, ridicule, mockery, irony, scorn, or contempt).

8. ' *Impassioned* ' (including all *very bold* pieces, and such violent passions as anger, defiance, revenge, &c.).

When selections are of a *mixed* character, — some passages ' matter-of-fact,' some ' bold,' some ' noble,' &c., — the *first* question must be asked as often as there is a marked change.

Having *clearly analyzed* any given example, we are ready intelligently to ask and answer the first *elocutionary* question, viz., How can we *read* the same so as to *express* with the voice the '*general spirit*' and the '*individual ideas*' with the '*relative importance*' of each? This brings us to the subject of —

VOCAL EXPRESSION.

Before analyzing the elements of vocal expression, let pupils be made to understand, as clearly as possible, this broad, general principle, viz., that EXPRESSION in *Nature* or *Art* depends on some kinds of *lights* and *shades*, as of color, or form, or sound.

Let them see that the clean *white wall* or the *blackboard* has *no expression*, just because it has but *one* shade of *one* color, while the painted *map* on the wall *expresses* something, because it has *different shades* of *various colors*.

They will then the more clearly understand that the true expression of thoughts and feelings in reading depends on using the right *lights* and *shades* of the *voice;* that a monotonous *tone* gives no more expression to the *ear* than the one monotonous color does to the eye.

All our lights and shades of expression in elocution are to be made out of the following : —

ELEMENTS OF VOCAL EXPRESSION.

1. '*Force*,' with all its natural variety, from moderate to louder or softer.

2. '*Time*,' with its changes from moderate to faster or slower movement, also with its longer or shorter *quantity* and *pauses*.

3. '*Slides*,' '*rising*,' and '*falling*,' and '*circumflex*,' and all these as moderate, or longer or shorter.

4. '*Pitch*,' with its variety of '*key-note*,' '*compass*,' and '*melody*.'

5. '*Volume*,' with more or less '*fulness*' of tone.

6. '*Stress*,' or the different *kinds* of force, as '*abrupt*,' or '*smooth*,' or as given to different *parts* of a syllable.

7. '*Quality*,' as '*pure*,' and resonant, or '*impure*,' and aspirated.

Let us now study and practise the principles for the right use of each one of these elements of vocal expression, in Part II.

PART II.

PRINCIPLES AND ILLUSTRATIONS OF THE ELEMENTS OF VOCAL EXPRESSION.

FORCE.

As in our analysis of the *spirit* and *sense* of each passage, we have always two quite different questions to ask, viz., What is the *general spirit*, and what the relative importance of the *individual ideas?* so in our analysis of each one of the *elements* of vocal expression, we have the same *general* and *individual* inquiries to make : —

1. What *general* degree of *force* will best express the 'general spirit' of the piece?

2. Taking this general force as our 'standard' degree of loudness or softness to be given to the *unemphatic* words, how much *additional* force must we give to the *emphatic* words, in order to bring out, in our reading, the relative importance of the different ideas?

PRINCIPLE FOR STANDARD FORCE.

Determine the 'standard force' for the unemphatic words by the 'kind' or 'general spirit' of the piece.

If the kind is 'unemotional,' the standard force is '*moderate.*'

If the kind is 'bold,' the standard force is '*loud.*'

If the kind is 'pathetic or subdued,' the standard force is '*soft.*'

PRINCIPLE FOR RELATIVE OR EMPHATIC FORCE.

Taking the 'standard force' for the *unemphatic* words, give *additional* force to the *emphatic* ideas, according to their *relative importance.*

> "Learning is better than wealth;
> Culture is better than learning;
> Wisdom is better than culture."

ANALYSIS.

The 'general spirit' or 'kind' is '*unemotional.*' The '*standard force*' is, therefore, '*moderate.*' The words "better" and "wealth" in the first line must have just enough *additional* force to distinguish them from the unemphatic words "is" and "than." "Learning" is *more important* than "wealth," and must have enough more force than "wealth" to express its relative importance. "Culture" is more important than "learning," and must therefore be read with more force. "Wisdom" is still more important than "culture," and must be read with still more force, to distinguish it as the *most* important of all.

Hence, to read this simple paragraph *naturally*, that is, to express distinctly the general spirit and the relative importance of the different ideas, we need *five distinct degrees of force.*

Let us mark the *least* degree of emphatic force by *italics*, the second by *small capitals*, the third by *large capitals*, the fourth by *larger capitals*, and *express* the same in reading.

> "LEARNING is *better* than *wealth;*
>
> CULTURE is better than LEARNING;
>
> **WISDOM** is better than CULTURE."

'Unemotional' examples for 'moderate' standard force.

1. "I am charged with *ambition.* The charge is *true,* and I GLORY in its truth. Who ever achieved anything GREAT in *letters, arts,* or *arms,* who was NOT *ambitious?* *Cæsar* was not *more ambitious* than *Cicero.* It was but in *another way.* ALL GREATNESS is born of *ambition.* Let the ambition be a NOBLE one, and who shall *blame* it?"

2. "The *plumage* of the *mocking-bird,* though none of the

homeliest, has nothing *gaudy* or *brilliant* in it, and, had he
nothing *else* to recommend him, would scarcely entitle him to
notice ; but his *figure* is *well-proportioned*, and even HANDSOME.
The *ease, elegance*, and *rapidity* of his *movements*, the *animation*
of his *eye*, and the INTELLIGENCE he displays in *listening*, and
laying up lessons from almost every species of the feathered
creation within his hearing, are really SURPRISING, and mark
the *peculiarity* of his genius."

3. "Three *poets*, in three *distant* ages born,
   Greece, Italy, and *England* did *adorn :*
   The *first* in MAJESTY of thought *surpassed ;*
   The *next* in GRACEFULNESS ; in BOTH, the *last*."

UNMARKED EXAMPLES.*

4. "Not enjoyment, and not sorrow,
   Is our destined end or way ;
   But to act, that each to-morrow
   Find us farther than to-day.

   "Let us, then, be up and doing,
   With a heart for any fate ;
   Still achieving, still pursuing,
   Learn to labor and to wait."

5. "In every period of life the acquisition of knowledge is
one of the most pleasing employments of the human mind.
But in youth there are circumstances which make it productive
of higher enjoyment. It is then that everything has the charm
of novelty, that curiosity and fancy are awake, and that the
heart swells with the anticipations of future eminence and
utility."

* Some examples, under Force, Time, and Slides, are given without elocutionary marks, that teachers and pupils may exercise their own judgment and
taste in analyzing and reading them according to the principles.

‘ Bold’ examples for ‘ loud’ standard force.

1. " Sir, we have done *everything* that *could* be done to *avert* the storm which is now coming on.· We have *petitioned ;* we have REMONSTRATED ; we have *supplicated;* we have *prostrated* ourselves before the *throne,* and have implored *its* interposition to ARREST the *tyrannical* hands of the *ministry* and *parliament.* Our *petitions* have been *slighted;* our *remonstrances* have produced ADDITIONAL *violence* and *insult;* our *supplications* have been *disregarded;* and we have been SPURNED, with *contempt,* from the foot of the throne ! "

2. " My friends, our *country must* be FREE ! The land
Is never *lost,* that has a *son* to *right* her,
And here are *troops* of sons, and LOYAL ones !
Strong in her *children* should a *mother* be :
Shall *ours* be HELPLESS, that has sons like US ?
God SAVE our NATIVE *land,* whoever pays
The ransom that redeems her ! Now what wait we ?
For *Alfred's* word to *move upon* the *foe ?*
UPON him then ! *Now think* ye on the things
You *most* do *love ! Husbands* and *fathers,* on
Their WIVES and CHILDREN ; *lovers* on their BELOVED ;
And ALL upon their COUNTRY ! "

3. " The gentleman, sir, has misconceived the spirit and tendency of Northern institutions. He is ignorant of Northern character. He has forgotten the history of his country. Preach insurrection to the Northern laborers ? Who are the Northern laborers ? The history of your country is their history. The renown of your country is their renown. The brightness of their doings is emblazoned on its every page. Where is Concord, and Lexington, and Princeton, and Trenton, and Saratoga, and Bunker Hill, but in the North ? And what, sir, has shed

an imperishable renown on the names of those hallowed spots, but the blood, and the struggles, the high daring, and patriotism, and sublime courage of Northern laborers? The whole North is an everlasting monument of the freedom, virtue, intelligence, and indomitable independence of Northern laborers. Go, sir, go preach insurrection to men like these!"

4. "Our Fatherland is in danger! Citizens! to arms! to arms! Unless the whole Nation rise up, as one man, to defend itself, all the noble blood already shed is in vain; and on the ground where the ashes of our ancestors repose the Russian knout will rule over an enslaved People! We have nothing to rest our hopes upon but a righteous God and our own strength. And if we do not put forth that strength, God will also forsake us. Hungary's struggle is no longer our struggle alone. It is the struggle of popular freedom against tyranny. In the wake of our victory will follow liberty to the Italians, Germans, Poles. With our fall goes down the star of freedom over all."

Examples of the 'subdued' or 'pathetic' kind for 'soft' standard force.

1. "Little Nell was *dead.* No *sleep* so *beautiful* and *calm,* so *free* from trace of *pain,* so *fair* to look upon. She seemed a creature FRESH from the hand of God, and *waiting* for the *breath* of *life;* not one who HAD *lived* and *suffered* DEATH. Her *couch* was dressed with here and there some *winter berries* and *green leaves,* gathered in a spot she had been used to *favor.* 'When I *die,* put *near* me something that has *loved* the LIGHT, and had the SKY *above it always.*' Those were her words."

2.   "But *Bozzaris* FELL,
          Bleeding at every *vein.*
          His few surviving comrades saw

His *smile,* when *rang* their *proud* HURRAH,
And the red field was *won :*
Then saw in *death* his eyelids *close*
Calmly, as to a *night's repose,*
Like *flowers* at *set* of *sun.*"

3. " I have known deeper wrongs. I, that speak to ye,
I had a brother once, a gracious boy,
Full of all gentleness, of calmest hope,
Of sweet and quiet joy, — there was the look
Of Heaven upon his face, which limners give
To the beloved disciple. How I loved
That gracious boy ! Younger by fifteen years,
Brother at once, and son ! He left my side,
A summer bloom on his fair cheeks, — a smile
Parting his innocent lips. In one short hour,
The pretty, harmless boy was slain ! "

4. " There is a calm for those who weep,
A rest for weary pilgrims found ;
They softly lie and sweetly sleep,
Low in the ground.

" The storm, that sweeps the wintry sky,
No more disturbs their deep repose
Than summer evening's latest sigh,
That shuts the rose."

' Soft force ' is also appropriate for the 'grave' kind of senti-ments, and 'loud force' for the 'joyous' and 'noble,' and 'very loud force' for the 'impassioned'; but since *other* elements of the voice, such as ' *time,*' ' *slides,*' ' *quality,*' &c., have more *char-acteristic prominence* than '*force*' in the finished expression of these classes, we shall be more likely to secure *naturalness* in the end, if we call attention *first* to the MOST *characteristic* elements.

TIME.

'*Time*' has the same *general* and *relative* use as 'Force.'

PRINCIPLE FOR STANDARD TIME.

Determine the 'standard time' by the 'general spirit' of the piece.

If the general spirit is 'unemotional,' the standard time is naturally '*moderate.*'

If the general spirit is 'animated or joyous,' the standard time is '*fast.*'

If the general spirit is 'grave,' 'subdued or pathetic,' or 'noble,' the standard time is '*slow.*'

PRINCIPLE FOR RELATIVE OR EMPHATIC TIME.

Taking the 'standard time' for the *unemphatic* words, give *additional* time to the *emphatic* ideas, according to their *relative importance.*

EXPLANATION.

'*Emphatic time*' has *two* forms. 1. That of actual sound, or '*quantity.*' 2. That of rest, or '*pause.*'

When an emphatic idea is found in a word whose accented syllable is *long*, give *most* of the emphatic time in long *quantity*, with only a short pause after the word. When the syllable to be emphasized is *short*, give to it only so much quantity as *good taste* in *pronunciation* will allow, and the *residue* of the required time in a *pause after* the word ; thus holding the attention of the mind on the idea for the *full time* demanded by the principle.

When *extraordinary* emphasis of time is required, *long pauses* must be *added* to *long quantity.*

Thus far 'time' harmonizes with 'force' in principle and practice. But 'time' is of additional value to us. It furnishes one of the primary requisites to all intelligible reading, viz. :—

APPROPRIATE PAUSES.

The first and great use of ' pauses ' is to *separate the ideas* from each other, so as to preserve distinctly to the eye on the written page, and to the ear in reading, the *individuality* of each, together with its *relation* to those *before* and *after* it.

Second, pauses are necessary to give the reader frequent opportunities for inhaling.

The grammatical pauses only imperfectly answer these purposes. But the additional *elocutionary* pauses which the *spirit* and *sense* may demand, are anticipated by our " Principle for relative or emphatic time," which makes *pauses* a natural *part* of *expressive emphasis* in reading.

PRINCIPLE FOR STANDARD PAUSES.

Determine the ' standard pause ' by the ' general spirit ' of the piece.

If the general spirit is ' unemotional,' the standard pause is ' *moderate.*'

If the general spirit is ' animated or joyous,' the standard pause is ' *short.*'

If the general spirit is ' grave,' or ' subdued or pathetic,' the standard pause is ' *long.*'

PRINCIPLE FOR RELATIVE PAUSES.

Give the ' standard pause ' after each distinct, unemphatic idea, and give additional time to the pauses after the *emphatic* and *independent* ideas, according to their *relative* importance and independence.

EXPLANATION.

As the ' standard time ' for the *movement* and *pauses* is usually the *same*, let one perpendicular line | be the mark for both. Let any additional number of lines indicate additional time, or *emphatic* ' *quantity* ' or ' *pauses.*' Let the half line Ꞌꞏ indicate a time *less* than the standard. This time is needed in reading properly all parenthetical clauses, which are, from their very nature, *less* important even than the *unemphatic* parts of the principal sentences.

'Unemotional' examples for 'moderate' standard time.

1. "The young man, | it is often said, | has *genius* || enough, | if he would only *study*. || Now the truth is, | as I shall take the liberty to state it, | that the *genius* || WILL ||| *study ;* || it is that | in the mind | which *does* || study : | that is the very *nature* || of it. | I care not to say | that it will always use *books*. || All *study* || is not *reading*, || any more than all *reading* || is *study*. || ATTENTION ||| it is, — | though other qualities belong to this transcendent power, — | ATTENTION |||| it is, | that is the very SOUL ||| of *genius ;.* || not the fixed *eye*, || not the poring over a *book*, || but the fixed THOUGHT." |||

ANALYSIS.

The piece is '*unemotional,*' and should be read, therefore, with '*moderate*' '*standard time*' for '*movement*' and '*pauses.*' "The young man" is unemphatic, and should be marked and read with the 'standard time.' The clause, "it is often said," is really parenthetical : it forms no essential part of the sense or construction of the principal sentence. It is for that reason of less importance than the unemphatic words of the principal sentence. It should therefore be read with *less* than 'moderate' or 'standard time.' The idea in "genius" is emphatic, and should be read with enough more time (as well as force) than "young man" to express its greater relative importance. The accented syllable is *long* in "genius." The emphatic time may be given, therefore, mostly in *quantity,* with a *short pause* after the word. "Enough" needs only the moderate pause after it, to separate it from the conditional idea, "if he would only study." "Study" is as emphatic as "genius," but the accented syllable is *short ;* hence, the emphatic time on this word must be given in *short quantity,* and a *longer pause* after it to fill out the time. "Now the truth is," requires 'moderate' time, as it is unemphatic. " As I shall take the liberty to state it," requires *less* than moderate *time* and *force*, as it is of less importance, being parenthetical. " That the genius " is emphatic, and demands more than moderate time. " Will " is still more important, and demands *three* lines to mark its relative time in reading. " Study " is emphatic in the first degree, and needs only *two* lines to mark its time. — Thus analyze all the following ideas and selections ; and mark, in reading them, the relative importance or emphasis of each, by the '*time*' as well as by the ' force' of the voice. Further on in the piece above, we come to the great positive idea, " attention," which must be doubly emphasized ; and as it is repeated for emphasis, it then demands *four* lines to mark its *superlative* importance.

There are few readers or speakers who make as good use of ' time' as of 'force.' Yet 'time' gives as expressive lights and shades as 'force,' and should be varied as much, according to the same principle. In reading ' grave,' ' subdued or pathetic,' and ' noble ' sentiments, *time* is far *more prominent* than *force*, and is thus a nobler element of emphasis. Let the example be read many times, to fix in the reader's mind the *principle*, and the *habit* of applying it correctly.

2. " What polish is to the diamond, manner is to the individual. It heightens the value and the charm. The manner is, in some sense, the mirror of the mind. It pictures and represents the thoughts and emotions within. We cannot always be engaged in expressive action. But even when we are silent, even when we are not in action, there is something in our air and manner, which expresses what is elevated, or what is low ; what is human and benignant, or what is coarse and harsh.

" The charm of manner consists in its simplicity, its grace, and its sincerity. How important the study of manner ! "

This example demands ' slower' standard time than the one above, because the '*general spirit*' is *nobler*. The emphatic *quantity* and *pauses* are proportionately longer.

3. " Such | was *Grace Darling*, || — one of the HEROINES |||
of *humanity*, — || whose name | is destined to *live* || as long
as the *sympathies* || and *affections* || of HUMANITY ||| *endure*. ||
Such calm | HEROISM ||| as *hers*, || — so *generously* || exerted for
the good | of *others*, — || is one of the NOBLEST ||| attributes of
the *soul* || of man. | It had no alloy of blind | *animal* || pas-
sion, | like the bravery of the *soldier* || on the field of *battle*, ||
but it was *spiritual*, || CELESTIAL, |||| and we may reverently
add, | GODLIKE." ||||

*Examples of the 'animated or joyous' kind, for 'fast' standard
time, and 'short' standard pauses.*

"THE VOICE OF SPRING.

1. "I come! || I come! ||| ye have called me | long! ||
I come | o'er the mountains || with light | and song! ||
Ye may trace | my step | o'er the wakening | earth, ||
By the winds || which tell | of the violet's || birth, |
By the primrose stars || in the shadowy grass, ||
By the green leaves || opening || as I pass. ||

"From the streams and founts I have loosed the chain,
They are sweeping on to the silvery main,
They are flashing down from the mountain brows,
They are flinging spray o'er the forest boughs,
They are bursting fresh from their sparry caves;
And the earth resounds with the joy of waves!"

2. "Then Fancy, || her magical | pinions | spread wide, ||
And bade the young dreamer | in ecstasy || rise; ||
Now, far, | far behind him, || the green waters || glide, |
And the cot | of his forefathers || blesses || his eyes. |

" The jessamine || clambers | in flower | o'er the thatch, |
    And the swallow || sings sweet || from her nest | in the .
    wall ; |
    All trembling | with transport, || he raises the latch, |
    And the voices | of loved ones || reply to his call." ||

3. " Every one is doubtful what course to take, — every
one || but Cæsar ! || He || causes the banner || to be erected, ||
the charge || to be sounded, | the soldiers at a distance | to be re-
called, — || all in a moment. | He runs | from place to place ; ||
his whole frame ||| is in action ; || his words, || his looks, || his
motions, || his gestures, || exhort his men | to remember | their
former valor. || He draws them up, | and causes the signal
to be given, — | all in a moment. | He seizes a buckler | from
one of the private men, — | puts himself || at the head | of his
broken troops, — || darts into the thick || of the battle, — ||
rescues || his legions, || and overthrows ||| the enemy ! " ||

' Grave' examples for ' slow' standard time.

1. "But where, || thought I, | is the crew? || Their struggle |
has long been over ; — || they have gone down | amidst the
roar of the tempest ; — || their bones lie whitening | in the cav-
erns of the deep. || Silence — ||| oblivion — |||| like the waves, ||
have closed over them ; || and no one can tell || the story of
their end. |||

"What sighs || have been wafted after that ship! || What
prayers || offered up | at the deserted fireside of home ! || How
often | has the mistress, || the wife, || and the mother || pored
over the daily news, || to catch some casual intelligence | of
this rover of the deep! || How has expectation || darkened |
into anxiety, — || anxiety | into dread, — ||| and dread || into
despair ! |||| Alas ! || not one | memento | shall ever return |
for love || to cherish. || All that shall ever be known, | is, |
that she sailed from her port, || and was never || heard of ||
more." ||||

' Grave' example for very ' slow time' and very ' long pauses.'

2. "It must‖ be so. ‖   Plato, ‖ thou reasonest well ! ‖
Else | whence | this pleasing hope, ‖ this fond desire, ‖
This longing ‖| after immortality ? ‖‖
Or whence | this secret dread ‖| and inward horror ‖|
Of falling into nought ? ‖‖   Why | shrinks the soul |
Back | on herself, ‖ and startles ‖ at destruction ? ‖‖
'T is the Divinity ‖| that stirs | within us : ‖
'T is Heaven ‖ itself ‖| that points out an hereafter, ‖
And intimates | Eternity ‖| to man. ‖
Eternity ! — ‖‖ thou pleasing, — ‖ dreadful thought !" ‖‖

' Pathetic' example for ' slow' standard time.

3. "Alas! ‖   my noble boy ! ‖‖ that thou | shouldst die ! ‖‖
Thou, ‖ who wert made | so beautifully fair ! ‖‖
That death ‖ should settle | in thy glorious eye, ‖‖
And leave his ‖ stillness ‖| in thy clustering hair ! ‖‖
How could he ‖ mark thee ‖‖ for the silent tomb, ‖‖
My proud | boy, ‖ Absalom !" ‖‖

SLIDES.

In perfectly natural speech, the voice rises or falls on each unemphatic syllable through the interval of *one tone only*, but on the accented syllable of an *emphatic* word it *rises* or *falls* MORE THAN ONE TONE.

This last is called the *inflection* or ' *slide*' of the voice. The ' slides' are thus a *part* of *emphasis*, and as they give the *right direction* and *limit* to ' force' and ' time,' they are the *crowning* part of perfect emphasis.

. When contrasted ideas, of equal importance, are coupled, nothing but the *contrasted slides* can give the proper *distinctive* emphasis. The slides also furnish to elocution its most ample and varied lights and shades of *emotional* expression.

These slides are ' rising,' marked thus ('); or ' falling,' marked thus (`); or both of these blended, in the ' rising' *circumflex,* and the 'falling' *circumflex,* marked respectively thus (∨) and thus (∧).

The 'rising' and 'falling' slides separate the great mass of ideas into *two distinct classes ;* the *first* comprising all the subordinate, or incomplete, or, as we prefer to name them, the *negative* ideas ; the *second* comprising all the principal, or complete, or, as we shall call them, the *positive* ideas.

The most *important* parts of what is spoken or written are those which affirm something *positively,* such as the *facts* and *truths asserted,* the *principles, sentiments,* and *actions enjoined,* with the *illustrations,* and *reasons,* and *appeals* which *enforce* them.

All these may properly be grouped into *one class,* because they *all* should have the *same kind* of slide in reading.

This class we call ' POSITIVE ideas.'

So all the other ideas which do *not* affirm or enjoin anything *positively,* which are *circumstantial* and *incomplete,* or in *open contrast* with the positive, all these ideas may be properly grouped into another *single class,* because they *all* should have the *same kind* of slide.

This class we call ' NEGATIVE ideas.'

Grant to the words ' positive' and ' negative' the *comprehensive* meaning here given to them, and let the distinction between the two classes be clearly made in the preparatory analysis, and it will be vastly easier to understand and teach this most complicated and difficult part of elocution, *the right use of the rising and falling slides.*

For, then, the *one simple principle* which follows will take the place, and preclude the use of, all the usual perplexing rules, with their many suicidal exceptions.

PRINCIPLES FOR RISING OR FALLING SLIDES.

POSITIVE ideas should have the *'falling'* slide ; NEGATIVE ideas should have the ' *rising'* slide.

Examples for the rising and falling slides.

" The war must go ȍn. We must fight it thróugh. And if the war must go ȍn, why put off lȍnger the declaration of

indepèndence ? That measure will strèngthen us. It will give
us chàracter abroad.

" The càusè will raise up àrmies ; the càuse will create nàvies.
The pèople, the pèople, if we are true to them, will carry ús,
and will carry themsèlves, gloriously thróugh this struggle. Sir,
the declaration will inspire the people with increased coúrage.
Instead of a long and bloody war for restorátion of prívileges,
for redréss of griévances, for chartered immúnities, held under
a British kíng, set before them the glorious object of entire
indepèndence, and it will breathe into them anèw the breath
of lìfe.

" Through the thick glóom of the présent, I see the brìghtness
of the fúture, as the sùn in heàven. We shall make this a glòrious, an immórtal day. When wé are in our gráves, our chìl-
dren will hònor it. They will cèlebrate it with thanksgìving,
with festìvity, with bònfires, and illuminàtions. On its annual
retúrn, they will shed tèars, cópious, gúshing tears, not of sub-
jéction and slávery, not of ágony and distréss, but of exultàtion,
of gràtitude, and of jóy."

QUESTIONS.

Questions, like other ideas, are *negative*, or *positive*, or compound, having *one* negative and *one* positive idea.

DIRECT QUESTIONS.

The *direct question* for *information affirms nothing.* Hence
it is read with the *rising* slide, not because it may be answered
by yes or no, but because it is in its nature *negative.*
The *answer* is *positive*, and, for that reason, is read with the
falling slide.

" Do you see that beautiful stár ? " " Yès."
" Isn't it splèndid ? "

The speaker is *positive*, in the last question, that his friend
will agree with him. This, and *all such,* must be read, therefore, with the *falling* slide.

" I said an èlder soldier, not a bétter.
Dìd I say better ? "

" He hath brought many captives home to Rome,
Whose ransoms did the gènéral coffers fill;
Did thìs in Cæsar seem ambìtious ? "

" You all did seè, that on the Lúpercal,
I thrìce presented him a kingly crown;
Which he did thrice refúse.   Was thìs ambìtion ? "

"Tell me, ye who tread the sods of yon sacred height, is
Wárren deád ?   Can you not stìll see him, not pále and prós-
trate, the blood of his gallant heárt pouring out of his ghastly
woúnd, but moving resplèndent over the field of hònor, with
the rose of heàven upon his cheèk, and the fire of lìberty in
his eyè ? "

" But whèn shall we be strónger ?   Will it be the next weék,
or the next yeàr ? "

This reading, with the *falling* slide on " *year,*" changes the
sense, as it makes *one* idea *positive,* and the answer must be
" next week," or " next year."   But *both* ideas are *negative* in
Henry's speech; both must have the *rising* slide, then, according to the principle.

" Will it be the next weék, or the next yeár ?   Will it be
when we are totally disármed, and when a British guárd shall
be stationed in every hoúse ? "

" Is thís a time to be gloómy and sád,
When our mother Náture laúghs around;
When even the deep blue heávens look glád,
And gládness breathes from the blóssoming ground ? "

" ' Will you ríde, in the cárriage, or on hórseback ? '   ' I prefer
to wàlk.' "

"'Will you reád to us, a piece of próse, or póetry?' 'Allow me to sìng instead.'"

"Will you study músic, or Frénch?"

All the ideas are *negative* in the last questions. Change the sense, and make *one* idea *positive* in each question, and we have *one falling* slide in each.

"Will you ride in the cárriage, or on hòrseback?"

"Will you read to us a piece of próse, or pòetry?"

"Will you study músic, or Frènch?"

INDIRECT QUESTIONS.

"When are you going to Eùrope?"

The prominent idea in this is not the real interrogative, the idea of *time* in "when," but the *positive* idea, "*You are going to Europe.*" Hence this, and *all such* questions must be read with the *falling* slide.

But if the *interrogative* is made the prominent and emphatic idea (as when, the answer not being heard, the question is repeated), the *rising* slide must be given.

"Whén are you going to Europe?"

"Why is the Fòrum cròwded?
What meàns this stìr in Rome?"

ADDRESS.

The *address* also is positive or negative. It is negative, and read with the *rising* slide or *suspension* of the voice, when it is only *formal* and *unemphatic;* as, "Friénds, I come not here to talk."

When *emphatic* it is *positive* and demands the *falling* slide, as in the respectful opening address to any deliberative body or public assembly. "*Mr. Prèsident,*" "*Ladies and Gèntle men.*"

POSITIVE ADDRESS AND QUESTIONS.

"Tell me, man of military science, in how many months were the Pilgrims all swept òff by the thirty savage tribes, enumerated within the early limits of New England? Tell me, politician, how long did this shadow of a colony, on which your convéntions and tréaties had not smíled, lànguish on the distant coast? Student of hìstory, compare for me the baffled projects, the abandoned adventures of other times; and find a pàrallel of thìs."

"Was it the winter's stòrm beating upon the houseless heads of women and children; was it hard làbor and spare meàls; — was it disèase, — was it the tòmahawk, — was it the deep malady of a blighted hòpe, a ruined ènterprise, and a broken heàrt, aching in its last moments at the recollection of the loved, and lèft beyond the sea; was it sóme or àll of these united that hurried this forsaken company to their mèlancholy fate?"

These questions must be read with the '*falling*' slide, to give the idea positively that each *one* of the enumerated causes was *sufficient* to produce the supposed result. The *surprise* is thus made all the *greater* in the next sentence, which must be read as an *earnest negative* with the *long* '*rising*' slide.

"And is it póssible that néither of these causes, that not áll combíned, were able to blást this bud of hópe? Is it pòssible that from the beginning so fèeble, so fràil, so worthy not so much of admirátion as of pìty, there has gone fọrth a prògress so stèady, a gròwth so wònderful, an expànsion so àmple, a reàlity so impòrtant, a pròmise yèt to be fulfilled, so glòrious!"

When *surprise* thus deepens into *astonishment*, as it frequently does in its climàx, the *interrogative* form should be changed to the *exclamatory*, which demands the *falling* slide.

"Partakers in every peril, in the glory shall we not be permitted to participate? And shall we be told as a requital that we are estranged from the noble country for whose salvation our life-blood was poured out!"

CONTRASTED SLIDES.

When ideas are contrasted in couples, the rising and falling slides must be contrasted in reading them. Contrasted slides may also sometimes be used for greater *variety* or *melody*.

EXAMPLE.

1. "Sínk or swìm, líve or dìe, survíve or pèrish, I give my hand and heàrt to this vote."

"But, whatever may be óur fate, be assured, be assured that this declaràtion will stànd. It may cost tréasure, and it may cost bl"od; but it will stànd, and it will richly compènsate for bòth."

"Suppose that you see, at once, all the hours of the day and all the seasons of the year, a morning of spring, and a morning of autumn, a night brilliant with stars, and a night obscure with clouds;—you will then have a more just notion of the spectacle of the universe. Is it not wondrous, that while you are admiring the sun plunging beneath the vault of the west, another observer is beholding him as he quits the region of the east, — in the same instant reposing, weary, from the dust of the evening, and awaking fresh and youthful, in the dews of morn!"

CIRCUMFLEX SLIDES.

Straight means *right*, crooked means *wrong:* hence *right* ideas demand the *right* or *straight* slides, while *wrong* or *crooked* ideas demand the *crooked* or '*circumflex slides.*'

PRINCIPLE.

All *sincere* and *earnest*, or, in other words, all *upright* and *downright* ideas demand the *straight*, or upright and downright slides.

All ideas which are *not* sincere or earnest, but are used in jest, or irony, in ridicúle, sarcasm, or mockery, in insinuation or double meaning, demand the *crooked* or '*circumflex slides.*'

The *last* part of the circumflex is usually the *longer*, and always the more *characteristic* part. Hence when the *last* part of this double slide *rises* it is called the '*rising* circumflex '; when the *last* part *falls*, it is called the '*falling* circumflex.'

The '*rising* circumflex' should be given to the *negative*, the '*falling* circumflex' to the *positive* ideas of jest, irony, &c. When these ideas are *coupled* in *contrast*, the circumflex *slides* must be in contrast also to express them.

Example of jest.

MARULLUS. Yòu, sir; what trade are you?

2D CITIZEN. Truly, sir, in respect of a fîne workman, I am but, as you would say, a côbbler.

MAR. But what tràde art thou? Answer me diréctly.

2D CIT. A trade, sir, that, I hope, I may use with a ṣafe cŏnscience; which is, indeed, sir, a mĕnder of bad sôles.

MAR. What tràde, thou knàve? thou naughty knave, what tràde?

2D CIT. Nay, I beseech you, sir, be not ŏut wïth me : yet, if you bê out, sir, I can mĕnd you.

MAR. What mean'st thou by thàt? Ménd me, thou saucy fellow?

2D CIT. Why, sir, côbble you.

FLAVIUS. Thou art a còbbler, árt thou?

2D CIT. Truly, sir, ăll that I live by is with the ăwl.

FLAV. But wherefore art not in thy shòp to-day? Why dost
thou lead these men about the streèts?

2D CIT. Truly, sir, to wear ŏut their shôes, to get myself
into more wôrk. But, indeed, sir, we make holiday, to see
Cœ'sar, and to rejoice in his trìumph.

In the *last sentence*, the citizen drops his *jesting*, and spēaks
in earnest; and therefore with the *straight* slides.

Examples of sarcasm and irony.

2. "Now, sir, what was the conduct of your own allies to
Poland? Is there a single atrocity of the French in Italy, in
Switzerland, in Egypt if you please, more unprincipled and
inhuman than that of Russia, Austria, and Prussia, in Poland?

"O, but you 'regrêtted the partition of Poland!' Yês,
regrêtted!—you regrêtted the violence, and that is àll you
did."

3. "They bŏast they come but to imprôve our state, enlârge
our thoughts, and frêe us from the yoke of êrror! Yês, thêy
will give enlightened frêedom to oûr minds, who are themsêlves
the slâves of passion, avarice, and pride! They offer us protêc-
tion! yês, súch protection as vúltures give to lambs — covering
and devouring them! Tell your invaders we seek nò change —
and least of all súch change as thêy would bring us!"

4. "Good Lord! when one man dies who wears a crown,
   How the earth trembles, — how the nations gape,
   Amazed and awed!—but when that one man's victims,
   Poor worms, unclothed in purple, daily die
   In the grim cell, or on the groaning gibbet,
   Or on the civil field, ye pitying souls
   Drop not one tear from your indifferent eyes!"

5. CASSIUS. Urge me no more! I shall forget myself;
Have mind upon your health; tempt me no further.

BRUTUS. Away, slight man !

CAS. Is't possible ?

BRU. Hear me, for I will speak.
Must I give way and room to your rash choler ?
Shall I be frightened when a madman stares ?

CAS. O ye gods ! ye gods ! Must I endure all this ?

BRU. All this ? Ay, more. Fret till your proud heart break ;
Go show your slaves how choleric you are,
And make your bondmen tremble ! Must I budge ?
Must I observe you ? Must I stand and crouch
Under your testy humor ?
You shall digest the venom of your spleen,
Though it do split you ; for, from this day forth,
I'll use you for my mirth, — yea, for my laughter,
When you are waspish.

CAS. Is it come to this !

BRU. You say you are a better soldier :
Let it appear so ; make your vaunting true,
And it shall please me well. For mine own part,
I shall be glad to learn of nobler men.

LENGTH OF SLIDES.

The *length of the slides* depends on the 'general spirit' or
'kind' of what is read.

PRINCIPLE.

If the general spirit is 'unemotional,' the slides are '*moderate.*'

If the general spirit is 'bold,' 'joyous,' or 'noble,' the slides
are '*long.*'

If the general spirit is 'subdued or pathetic' or 'grave,' the
slides are '*short.*'

Examples for the ' moderate' slide, or in the definite language of music, the " Third."

" Can I speak with you a móment ? "   " Cèrtainly."

" The ancient Spàrtans were not less remarkable for their bràvery in the field of báttle, than for brevity and wìt in theii ànswers. We have a memorable instance of their national spírit, in the reply of the old wàrrior who was told that the arrows of the Persian host flew so thick as to darken the sùn. ' So much the bètter,' was his answer ; ' we shall enjoy the advantage of fighting in the shàde.' "

Examples for the ' long' slide, or the " Fifth."

" What but lìbèrty
Through the famed course of thirteen hundred yèars,
Alòof hath held invàsion from your hìlls,
And sànctified their nàme ?   And wíll ye, wíll ye
Shrínk from the hopes of the expecting wórld,
Bid your high hónors stóop to foreign ínsult,
And in one hóur give up to ínfamy
The harvest of a thousand yéars of glóry ?
Dìe — àll first ?   Yès, die by pìècemeal !
Leave not a lìmb o'er which a Dàne can trìumph ! "

" True courage but from opposition gròws,
And what are fìfty, what a thoúsand slâves,
Matched to the virtue of a sìngle arm
That strikes for lìberty ? that strikes to save
His fièlds from fìre, his ìnfants from the swòrd,
And his large hònors from eternal ìnfamy ? "

" Ye men of Sweden, wherefore are ye come ?
See ye not yonder, how the locusts swarm,
To drink the fountains of your honor up,
And leave your hills a desert ? Wretched men !
Why came ye forth ? Is this a time for sport ?

Or are ye met with song and jovial feast,
To welcome your new guests, your Danish visitants?
To stretch your supple necks beneath their feet
And fawning lick the dust?   Go, go, my countrymen,
Each to your several mansions, trim them out,
Cull all the tedious earnings of your toil,
To purchase bondage. — O, Swedes! Swedes!
Heavens! are ye men and will ye suffer this? —
There was a time, my friends, a glorious time!
When, had a single man of your forefathers
Upon the frontier met a host in arms,
His courage scarce had turned ; himself had stood,
Alone had stood, the bulwark of his country."

Example for the ' short' slide, or the " Minor Third."

"Dear, gentle, patient, noble Nell was dèad.   Her little
bírd, — a poor, slight thing the pressure of a finger would have
crúshed, — was stirring nimbly in its cáge, and the strong
heart of its child-mìstress was mute and mòtionless forever!

"Sórrow was déad, indeed, in her; but pèace and perfect
hàppiness were bòrn, — imaged — in her tranquil beauty and
profound repòse.

"Waking, she never wandered in her mind but once, and
that was at beautiful músic, which, she said, was in the aìr!
God knóws.   It máy have been.

"Opening her eyes at last from a very quiet sléep, she
begged that they would kìss her once agaìn.   That done, she
turned to the old màn, with a lovely smìle upon her fáce, —
such, they said, as they had never séen, and never could for-
gét, — and clung, with both her arms, about his nèck.   She
had never múrmured or compláined ; but with a qúiet mind,
and mánner quite unáltered, — save that she every day became
more eárnest and more gráteful to them, — faded like the light
upon the summer's evèning."

P.ITCH.

1. The '*standard pitch*' or '*key-note.*'   2. The '*relative pitch*' or '*melody.*'

The *middle* pitch is the *natural key-note* for 'unemotional,' 'bold,' and 'noble' pieces. A *higher* pitch is the *natural key-note* for 'animated and joyous,' 'subdued or pathetic,' and 'impassioned' pieces. A *lower* pitch is required for 'grave' pieces.

The middle or conversational pitch must be used for *all* 'kinds' when pupils have not the requisite compass or cultivation of voice to read *naturally* on a *higher* or a *lower* 'key.'

But appropriate variety of pitch on the successive words and syllables is one of the most essential and beautiful parts of good reading. In perfect elocution, it adds to the eloquence of *expressive emphasis* the *musical* charm of '*natural melody.*'

NATURAL MELODY

Is produced in part by that agreeable modulation of *all* the elements of expression, which the varied sense and feeling demand, yet it chiefly depends on a pleasing *variation* of the *radical* or *opening pitch*, on successive syllables.

PRINCIPLE.

1. Not *more* than *two* or *three consecutive syllables* should be given on the *same tone* of the musical scale.

2. Natural melody demands that this frequent change of pitch on the unemphatic syllables shall be only *one tone* at a time.

The unemphatic syllables form a kind of *flexible ladder* connecting the emphatic ideas, up and down which we must glide *tone* by *tone*, so as to be in the *right place* to give the *longer slides* on the emphatic words without an unmelodious break in the natural current of the voice, which should flow on smoothly through all changes (unless there is an *abrupt break* in the *ideas*), just as a *good road* runs on over ever-varying hills and vales without once losing its *smooth continuity.*

Melody demands that the pitch on *consecutive emphatic words* also be agreeably varied. Our limited space will not allow us to mark the many possible permutations of *pitch,* which may constitute natural melody. We will only repeat the important general directions. *Avoid monotony,* by giving at most only *two* or *three consecutive syllables,* on the *same tone.*

Avoid making *unnatural* changes of pitch, of *more* than *one* tone at a time.

Glide up the scale on the *negative* ideas, so that you will have *room above* the *key-note,* to *slide down easily* on the *positive* ideas.

COMPASS.

The *compass* of voice which should be used also depends on the 'spirit' of the piece.

The most 'joyous' and most 'impassioned' demand the widest range of pitch, and the greatest natural variety.

The 'unemotional' demands only moderate compass. The 'grave' demands still *less* variety and compass. And when the 'grave' deepens into *supernatural awe* or *horror,* by the same analogy, we may infer that *natural variety* or melody gives place to an *unnatural sameness* of utterance, with just that *little* variety of *all* the vocal elements which is necessary to express the sense at all.

Example for 'middle pitch' and 'moderate compass.'

"It is these which I love and venerate in England. I should feel ashamed of an enthusiasm for Italy and Greece, did I not also feel it for a land like this. In an American, it would seem to me degenerate and ungrateful, to hang with passion upon the traces of Homer and Virgil, and follow without emotion the nearer and plainer footsteps of Shakespeare and Milton."

'Joyous' example for 'higher pitch' and 'wider compass.'

"There was a sound of revelry by night,
　And Belgium's capital had gathered then

Her beauty and her chivalry ; and bright ·
    The lamps shone o'er fair women and brave men.
A thousand hearts beat happily, and when
    Music arose with its voluptúous swell,
Soft eyes looked love to eyes which spake again,
    And all went merry as a marriage-bell."

*'Grave' example for 'lower pitch' and less than 'moderate
compass.'*

" And, — when I am forgotten, as I shall be,
And sleep in dull cold marble, where no mention
Of me more must be heard of, — say I taught thee ;
Say, Wolsey, that once trod the ways of glory,
And sounded all the depths and shoals of honor,
Found thee a way, out of his wreck, to rise in,.
A sure and safe one, though thy master missed it.
Mark but my fall, and *that* that ruined me.
Cromwell, I charge thee, fling away ambition :
By that sin fell the angels ; how can man then,
The image of his Maker, hope to win by 't ?
Let all the ends thou aim'st at be thy country's,
Thy God's, and truth's : then, if thou fall'st, O Cromwell !
Thou fall'st a blessed martyr ! "

VOLUME.

'Full volume' is the most essential element in the truthful
expression of *'noble'* sentiment.

1. " Mìnd is the nòblest part of man ; and of *mínd*, vìrtue
is the noblest *distìnction*. Honest màn, in the ear of *Wísdom*,
is a *grànder* name, is a more *hígh-sounding* title, than *peer* of
the *réalm*, or *prince* of the *blóod*. According to the eternal
rules of *celéstial* precedency, in the *immortal heraldry* of *Náture*
and of *Héaven*, vìrtue takes place of *all* things. It is the
nobility of Àngels ! It is the majesty of GOD ! "

In addition to 'full volume,' 'noble' pieces demand slow time, or long quantity and pauses, long slides, and loud but smooth-swelling force on the emphatic words. *Full volume* distinguishes *manly* sentiments from the *thin* or *fine* tone of *child-like* emotions.

> 2. " But strew his ashes to the wind,
> Whose sword or voice has served mankind.
> And is he dead whose glorious mind
> Lifts thine on high?
> To live in hearts we leave behind,
> Is not to die.

> " Is 't death to fall for Freedom's right?
> He's dead alone that lacks her light!
> And Murder sullies in Heaven's sight
> The sword he draws : —
> What can alone ennoble fight?
> A noble cause! "

STRESS.

Stress is not the *degree* but the *kind* of emphatic force we use. The *same degree* of loudness may be given to a syllable *abruptly* and *suddenly*, as in sharp command, or *smoothly* and *gradually*, as in the noble examples given above. This *sudden* and *harsh* kind of force we will call ' *abrupt stress* '; the other, ' *smooth stress.* '

PRINCIPLE.

' *Abrupt stress* ' should be given to all *abrupt* or *harsh* ideas, and pleasant or ' *smooth stress* ' to all *good* or *pleasant* ideas.

Mere command is abrupt; indignation, anger, defiance, revenge, &c., are all *abrupt* in their very nature; and, therefore, must be read with the ' abrupt stress.'

ABRUPT STRESS.

1. *Impatient command.*

" *Hènce!* *hòme,* you *ìdle* creatures, get you *hòme.*
You *blòcks,* you STÒNES, you WÒRSE than *sènseless* things !
Be *gòne !*
Run to your *hoùses,* fall upon your *knèes,*
Pràj to the *gods* to *intermìt* the PLAGUE
That *needs must light* on this *ingràtitude.*"

The force must be thrown with an abrupt *jerk* on the emphatic
syllables.

2. *Anger.* (*Loud as well as 'abrupt' force and 'long
slides.'*)

" CASSIUS. That you have wronged me doth appear in this ;
You have condemned and noted Lucius Pella,
For taking bribes here of the Sardians ;
Wherein, my letter, praying on his side,
Because I knew the man, was slighted off.
BRUTUS. You wronged yourself to write in such a case.
CAS. In such a time as this it is not meet
That every nice offence should bear its comment.
BRU. Let me tell you, Cassius, you yourself
Are much condemned to have an itching palm ;
To sell and mart your offices for gold
To undeservers.
CAS. I an itching palm ?
You know that you are Brutus that speak this,
Or, by the gods, this speech were else your last.
BRU. The name of Cassius honors this corruption,
And chastisement does therefore hide his head.
CAS. Chastisement ?
BRU. Remember March, the ides of March remember.
Did not great Julius bleed for justice' sake ?

What villain touched his body, that did stab,
And not for justice? What! shall one of us,
That struck the foremost man of all this world,
But for supporting robbers, — shall we now
Contaminate our fingers with base bribes,
And sell the mighty space of our large honors,
For so much trash as may be grasped thus?
I had rather be a dog, and bay the moon,
Than such a Roman."

3. *Defiance.* (*'Very ' abrupt' and ' loud,' with ' long slides.'*)

"I have returned, *nót* as the right honorable member has
said, to raise another *stórm,* — I have returned to *protect* that
constitùtion, of which I was the párent and the foúnder, from
the *assassinàtion* of *such* men as the honorable *gèntleman* and
his unworthy *assòciates.* They are *corrùpt* — they are SEDI-
TIOUS — and they, at this very *mòment,* are in a CONSPIRACY
against their *coùntry!* Here I stand for *impeachment* or *trìal!*
I *dàre* accusation! I DEFY the honorable *gèntleman!* I *defy*
the GÒVERNMENT! I *defy* their whole PHALANX! Let them
come *fòrth!* I tell the ministers I will neither give *thém* quarter,
nor *tàke* it!"

4. *Indignation.*

"Who is the man, that, in addition to the disgraces and
mischiefs of the war, has dared to authorize and associate to
our arms the tomahawk and scalping-knife of the savage? —
to call into civilized alliance the wild and inhuman inhabitant of
the woods? — to delegate to the merciless Indian the defence
of disputed rights, and to wage the horrors of his barbarous
war against our brethren? My lords, we are called upon as
members of this house, as men, as Christian men, to protest
against such horrible barbarity."

SMOOTH STRESS.

All pleasant and good ideas demand '*smooth stress*' or force, *free* from all *abruptness*.

In 'joyous' pieces, when the *time* is *fast*, the stress must be given with a *lively*, SPRINGING *swell* of the voice, which throws the *force* smoothly on the middle of the sound.   Hence it is called the '*median*' stress.

'*Animated and joyous*' *examples for smooth stress.*

1.   " His cares flew away,
And vísions of hàppiness dànced o'er his mind.

" He dreamed of his hòme, of his dear nàtive bowers,
    And pléasures that waited on life's merry mòrn ;
While memory each scene gayly covered' with flówers,
    And restòred every róse, but secréted its thòrn."

In the following example of ' noble,' *manly* joy, the happy median stress swells with the same smooth, springing force as above, but with more fulness and longer *quantity* and *pauses*.

2. "Fellow Citizens,— I congratulate you, — I give you joy, on the return of this anniversary. I see, before and around me, a mass of faces, glowing with cheerfulness and patriotic pride. This anniversary animates and gladdens and unites all American hearts.   Every man's heart swells within him, — every man's port and bearing becomes somewhat more proud and lofty, as he remembers that seventy-five years have rolled away, and that the great inheritance of liberty is still his ; his, undiminished and unimpaired ; his, in all its original glory ; his to enjoy, his to protect, and his to transmit to future generations."

'*Subdued*' *example for gentle but happy median or smooth stress.*

" At last, Malibran came ; and the child sat with his glance riveted upon her glorious face. Could he believe that the grand lady, all blazing with jewels, and whom everybody seemed to worship, would really sing his little song? Breathless he waited; — the band, the whole band, struck up a little plaintive melody. He knew it, and clapped his hands for joy.

"And oh! how she sung it! It was so simple, so mournful, so soul-subduing; — many a bright eye dimmed with tears; and nought could be heard but the touching words of that little song, — oh! so touching!

"Little Pierre walked home as if he were moving on the air. What cared he for money now? The greatest singer in all Europe had sung his little song, and thousands had wept at his grief.

"Thus she, who was the idol of England's nobility, went about doing good. And in her early, happy death, when the grave-damps gathered over her brow, and her eyes grew dim, he who stood by her bed, his bright face clothed in the mourning of sighs and tears, and smoothed her pillow, and lightened her last moments by his undying affection, was the little Pierre of former days, — now rich, accomplished, and the most talented composer of his day."

'Noble' example for prolonged, full-swelling median or smooth stress.

"We must forget all feelings save the one;
We must behold no object save our country; —
And only look on death as beautiful,
So that the sacrifice ascend to Heaven,
And draw down freedom on her evermore.
'But if we fail?' They never fail, who die
In a great cause! The block may soak their gore;
Their heads may sodden in the sun; their limbs
Be strung to city gates and castle walls; —
But still their spirit walks abroad. Though years

Elapse, and others share as dark a doom,
They but augment the deep and sweeping thoughts
Which overpower all others, and conduct
The world, at last, to freedom!"

Examples for the longest 'quantity' and fullest 'swell' of the
median or smooth stress.

"O liberty! O sound once delightful to every Roman ear!
O sacred privilege of Roman citizenship! once sacred, — now
trampled on!"

" Ye crags and peaks, I'm with you once again!
O sacred forms, how proud you look!
How high you lift your heads into the sky!
How huge you are! how mighty and how free!
          " Ye guards of liberty,
I'm with you once again."

          " The land that bore you — O!
Do honor to her! Let her glory in
Your breeding."

" These are Thy glorious works, Parent of Good.
Almighty! Thine this universal frame,
Thus wondrous fair! Thyself how wondrous, then!"

Example for 'noble' but happy 'median stress.'

"The Lord is my shepherd; I shall not want.
"He maketh me to lie down in green pastures; He leadeth
me beside the still waters. He restoreth my soul."

QUALITY OF VOICE.

Quality of voice is '*pure*' or '*impure*.'
It is '*pure*' when *all* the breath used is *vocalized*.
It is '*impure*' or *aspirated* when only a *part* of the breath is
vocalized.

PRINCIPLE.

'Pure quality' should be used to express all *good* and *agreeable* ideas.

'Impure quality,' or *aspirated,* should be used to express all *bad* or *disagreeable ideas.*

Examples of 'impure quality.'

Painful earnestness or anxiety demands this *'aspirated quality'* with *'abrupt stress.'*

1. " Take care ! your very life is endangered ! "

2. " Oh ! 'twas a fearsome sight ! Ah me !
   A deed to shudder at, — not to see."

3. " While thronged the citizens with terror dumb,
   Or whispering with white lips, 'The foe! they come, they
   come ! ' "

4. " He springs from his hammock, he flies to the deck, —
   Amazement confronts him with images dire, —
   Wild winds and mad waves drive the vessel a wreck :
   The masts fly in splinters, the shrouds are on fire !

" Like mountains the billows tremendously swell :
   In vain the lost wretch calls on mercy to save ;
   Unseen hands of spirits are ringing his knell,
   And the death-angel flaps his broad wing o'er the wave."

Extreme aspiration should mark the *fear* and *horror* in the following words of Macbeth.

5.   " I'll go no more :
   I am afraid to think what I have done :
   Look on't again I dare not."

Strong aspiration and 'abrupt stress.'

6. " I am astonished, shocked, to hear such principles confessed, — to hear them avowed in this house, or in this country ; — principles equally unconstitutional, inhuman, and unchristian ! "

'Bold' and 'impassioned' examples for very 'abrupt stress' and 'aspirated quality' on the emphatic words.

7. "It was the act of a coward, who raises his arm to strike, but has not the courage to give the blow! I will not call him villain, because it would be unparliamentary, and he is a privy councillor. I will not call him fool, because he happens to be chancellor of the exchequer. But I say he is one who has abused the privilege of parliament and freedom of debate, to the uttering of language which, if spoken out of the house, I should answer only with a blow! I care not how high his situation, how low his character, or how contemptible his speech; whether a privy councillor or a parasite, my answer would be a blow!"

8. "The wretch, who, after having seen the consequences of a thousand errors, continues still to blunder, and whose age has only added obstinacy to stupidity, is surely the object of either abhorrence or contempt, and deserves not that his gray hairs should secure him from insult."

9. "If ye are beasts, then stand here like fat oxen waiting for the butcher's knife."

This quality of voice demands that the *aspirates* and the *less* resonant *consonants* be made very *prominent* in the enunciation, while the purer vowels and the liquid, pleasant consonants reserve their prominence till *pure* tone is required.

All examples of 'aspirated quality' require abrupt stress.

'Contemptuous and ironical' example.

10. "But base ignoble slaves, — slaves to a horde
Of petty tyrants, feudal despots, lords
Rich in some dozen paltry villages, —
Strong in some hundred spearmen, — only great
In that strange spell — a name."

Examples of 'pure quality.'

1. "That which befits us, imbosomed in beauty and wonder

as we are, is cheerfulness and courage, and the endeavor to realize our aspirations."

Example of 'pure tone,' with lively median stress.

2. "It is now sixteen or seventeen years since I saw the Queen of France, then the Dauphiness, at Versailles, and surely never lighted on this orb, which she hardly seemed to touch, a more delightful vision.

"I saw her just above the horizon, decorating and cheering the elevated sphere she just began to move in, glittering like the morning-star, full of life, and splendor, and joy."

'Lower pitch' and 'slower time.' 'Long quantity,' and pro-longed median stress.

3. "O! what a revolution! and what a heart must I have to contemplate without emotion that elevation and that fall! Little did I dream that I should have lived to see such disasters fallen upon her, in a nation of gallant men, in a nation of men of honor, and of cavaliers! I thought ten thousand swords must have leaped from their scabbards, to avenge even a look that threatened her with insult.

"But the age of chivalry is gone, and the glory of Europe is extinguished forever."

The following selection from Shelley's "To a Skylark," is full of rapturous beauty, and requires the '*purest* tone' and the smoothest and happiest 'median stress,' prolonged with swelling fulness on the emphatic words : —

4.   "Hail to thee, blithe spirit, —
          Bird thou never wert, —
        That from heaven, or near it,
         Pourest thy full heart
In profuse strains of unpremeditated art.

       "Higher still and higher
         From the earth thou springest ;
        Like a cloud of fire,

The blue deep thou wingest,
And singing still dost soar, and soaring ever singest.

" In the golden lightning
Of the sunken sun,
O'er which clouds are brightening,
Thou dost float and run,
Like an unbodied joy whose race is just begun.

" All the earth and air
With thy voice is loud,
As, when night is bare,
From one lonely cloud
The moon rains out her beams, and heaven is overflowed.

" What thou art, we know not ;
What is most like thee ?
From rainbow clouds there flow not
Drops so bright to see,
As from thy presence showers a rain of melody.

" Better than all measures
Of delightful sound,
Better than all treasures
That in books are found,
Thy skill to poet were, thou scorner of the ground !

" Teach me half the gladness
That thy brain must know,
Such harmonious madness
From my lips would flow,
The world should listen then, as I am listening now."

'Noble' example for 'pure tone,' to be given also with full 'median stress.'

" We wish that this column, rising towards heaven among
the pointed spires of so many temples dedicated to God, may
contribute also to produce, in all minds, a pious feeling of de-

pendence and gratitude. We wish, finally, that the last object on the sight of him who leaves his native shore, and the first to gladden him who revisits it, may be something which shall remind him of the liberty and glory of his country. Let it rise till it meet the sun in his coming ; let the earliest light of morning gild it, and parting day linger and play upon its summit."

'Subdued examples' for very soft force, 'short slides,' gentle 'median stress,' and the 'purest quality.'

" I thought to pass away before, and yet alive I am ;
And in the fields all round I hear the bleating of the lamb.
How sadly, I remember, rose the morning of the year !
To die before the snowdrop came, and now the violet's here.
O, sweet is the new violet, that comes beneath the skies,
And sweeter is the young lamb's voice to me that cannot rise,
And sweet is all the land about, and all the flowers that blow,
And sweeter far is death than life to me that long to go.

" O look ! the sun begins to rise, the heavens are in a glow ;
He shines upon a hundred fields, and all of them I know.
O sweet and strange it seems to me, that ere this day is done,
The voice that now is speaking may be beyond the sun —
Forever and forever ; all in a blessed home —
And there to wait a little while till you and Effie come —
To lie within the light of God, as I lie upon your breast —
And the wicked cease from troubling and the weary are at rest."

'Joyous' example for 'pure quality' and happy 'median stress.'

" And what is so rare as a day in June ?
Then, if ever, come perfect days ;
Then Heaven tries the earth if it be in tune,
And over it softly her warm ear lays :

Whether we look, or whether we listen,
We hear life murmur, or see it glisten;
Every clod feels a stir of might,
    An instinct within it that reaches and towers,
And, groping blindly above it for light,
    Climbs to a soul in grass and flowers;
The little bird sits at his door in the sun,
    Atilt like a blossom among the leaves,
And lets his illumined being o'errun
    With the deluge of summer it receives."

A striking example of *both qualities* may be taken from the dialogue between "Old Shylock" and "Portia." The tones of Shylock's voice, to express his *spite* and *revenge*, must be marked by the most *abrupt* 'stress' and '*aspirated* or *impure quality;*' while the beautiful sentiments of Portia demand the '*smoothest stress*' and '*purest quality.*'

> "PORTIA. Do you confess the bond?
>
> ANTONIO. I do.
>
> POR. Then must the Jew be merciful.
>
> SHYLOCK. On what compulsion must I? Tell me that.
>
> POR. The quality of mercy is not strained;
> It droppeth as the gentle rain from heaven
> Upon the place beneath: it is twice blessed;
> It blesseth him that gives and him that takes:
> 'Tis mightiest in the mightiest: it becomes
> The throned monarch better than his crown:
> It is enthroned in the hearts of kings,
> It is an attribute to God himself,
> And earthly power doth then show likest God's,
> When mercy seasons justice."

———————

Having thus treated of, and illustrated with various kinds of pieces, *each one* of the elements of elocution, *separately,* let us now finish our work by learning how *all* these separate elements *unite together* and *blend* in the natural expression of *each* 'kind' of sentiment.

'Unemotional' pieces should have 'moderate' 'standard force' and 'time' and 'slides' and 'volume,' 'middle pitch,' 'smooth stress,' and 'pure quality' of voice.

Unemotional example.

"There is something nobly simple and pure in a taste for the cultivation of forest trees. It argues, I think, a sweet and generous nature, to have a strong relish for the beauties of vegetation, and a friendship for the hardy and glorious sons of the forest. He who plants an oak looks forward to future ages, and plants for posterity. Nothing can be less selfish than this. He cannot expect to sit in its shade and enjoy its shelter; but he exults in the idea that the acorn which he has buried in the earth shall grow up into a lofty pile, and shall keep on flourishing and increasing and benefiting mankind, long after he shall have ceased to tread his paternal fields."

'Bold' pieces should have 'loud' 'standard force,' 'long slides,' 'moderate time,' with long quantity on the emphatic syllables, 'middle pitch,' 'abrupt stress,' and slightly 'aspirated quality.'

Bold example.

" Who, then, caused the strife
That crimsoned Naseby's field and Marston's Moor?
It was the Stuart ; — so the Stuart fell !
A victim, in the pit himself had digged !
He died not, sirs, as hated kings have died,
In secret and in shade, — no eye to trace
The one step from their prison to their pall :
He died in the eyes of Europe, — in the face
Of the broad heaven ; amidst the sons of England,
Whom he had outraged ; by a solemn sentence,
Passed by a solemn court. Does this seem guilt?
You pity Charles ! 'tis well ; but pity more
The tens of thousand honest humble men,
Who, by the tyranny of Charles compelled
To draw the sword, fell, butchered in the field ! "

'Animated or joyous' pieces should have 'fast time,' lively, springing 'median stress,' 'pure quality,' 'long slides,' 'high pitch,' and 'loud force.'

Joyous example.

" You must wake and call me early, call me early, mother dear,
To-morrow'll be the happiest time of all the glad New-Year;
Of all the glad New-Year, mother, the maddest, merriest day ;
For I'm to be Queen o' the May, mother, I'm to be Queen o'
    the May.

" I sleep so sound all night, mother, that I shall never wake,
If you do not call me loud when the day begins to break :
But I must gather knots of flowers, and buds and garlands
    gay,
For I'm to be Queen o' the May, mother, I'm to be Queen o'
    the May."

'Subdued or pathetic' pieces should have 'soft force,' 'short (or minor) slides,' 'slow time,' gentle 'median stress,' 'pure quality,' 'high pitch,' and less than 'moderate volume.'

Subdued or pathetic example.

" If you're waking, call me early, call me early, mother dear,
For I would see the sun rise upon the glad New-Year.
It is the last New-Year that I shall ever see,
Then you may lay me low i' the mould, and think no more of me.

" To-night I saw the sun set ! he set and left behind
The good old year, the dear old time, and all my peace of mind,
And the New-Year's coming up, mother, but I shall never see
The blossom on the blackthorn, the leaf upon the tree."

'Grave' pieces should have 'low pitch,' 'slow time,' with 'long quantity and pauses,' 'full volume,' 'soft force,' and 'short slides'—also 'smooth stress' and 'pure quality' when the ideas are *reverential* or *solemn merely*—but more or less

'abrupt stress' and 'aspirated quality' when characterized by
fear or *aversion,* as in 'dread,' 'awe,' and 'horror.'

Grave example.

" Come to the bridal chamber, — Death !
 Come to the mother, when she feels
 For the first time her first-born's breath ;
 Come when the blessed seals
 That close the pestilence are broke,
 And crowded cities wail its stroke ;
 Come in Consumption's ghastly form,
 The earthquake shock, the ocean storm,
 Come when the heart beats high and warm
 With banquet-song and dance and wine, —
 And thou art terrible ! the tear, —
 The groan, — the knell, — the pall, — the bier,
 And all we know, or dream, or fear,
 Of agony are thine."

'Noble' pieces should have 'full-swelling volume' and
'median stress,' with 'long quantity' and 'long slides,' 'loud
force,' 'pure quality,' and 'middle pitch.'

Noble example.

" But to the hero, when his sword
 Has won the battle for the free,
 Thy voice sounds like a prophet's word,
 And in its hollow tones are heard
 The thanks of millions yet to be.
 Bozzaris ! with the storied Brave
 Greece nurtured in her glory's time,
 Rest thee ! there is no prouder grave,
 Even in her own proud clime.
 We tell thy doom without a sigh ;
 For thou art Freedom's now and Fame's, —
 One of the few, the immortal names,
 That were not born to die ! "

Both '*ludicrous*' and '*sarcastic*' pieces should have long 'circumflex slides' and 'compound' 'abrupt stress,' 'long quantity and pauses' on the emphatic words; but *punning* and *raillery*, when good-natured, should have a 'higher pitch,' 'faster time,' and 'purer quality' than belongs to sarcasm, which should have the 'middle pitch,' 'aspirated quality,' and rather 'slow time.' With both kinds the 'force' changes from 'moderate' to louder with the boldness of the spirit.

In the following example the part of Sir Peter Teazle should be read with strongly 'aspirated quality' and 'abrupt stress,' while the half-laughing raillery of Lady T. should have the 'pure quality' and 'tremulous stress' mingled with the 'compound,' and 'higher pitch,' and 'less volume.'

Ludicrous or sarcastic example.

"SIR PETER. Very well, ma'am, very well — so a husband is to have no influence, no authority?

LADY T. Authority! No, to be sure : — if you wanted authority over me, you should have adopted me, and not married me; I am sure you were old enough.

SIR P. Old enough! — ay, there it is. Well, well. Lady Teazle, though my life may be made unhappy by your temper, I'll not be ruined by your extravagance.

LADY T. My extravagance! Sir Peter, am I to blame because flowers are dear in cold weather? You should find fault with the climate, and not with me. For my part, I'm sure, I wish it was spring all the year round, and that roses grew under our feet !

SIR P. Zounds! madam — if you had been born to this, I shouldn't wonder at your talking thus; but you forget what your situation was when I married you.

LADY T. No, no, I don't; 'twas a very disagreeable one, or I should never have married you. Sir Peter! would you have me be out of the fashion?

SIR P. The fashion, indeed! What had you to do with the fashion before you married me?

LADY T. For my part, I should think you would like to have your wife thought a woman of taste.

SIR P. Ay, there again — taste. Zounds! madam, you had no taste when you married me!

LADY T. That's very true, indeed, Sir Peter; and after having married you I should never pretend to taste again, I allow. But now, Sir Peter, since we have finished our daily jangle, I presume I may go to my engagement at Lady Sneerwell's.

SIR P. Ay, there's another precious circumstance — a charming set of acquaintance you have made there."

Example of bitter irony and sarcasm closing with the impassioned kind.

" I speak not to you, Mr. Renwick, of your own outcast condition ; — perhaps you delight in the perils of martyrdom : I speak not to those around us, who, in their persons, their substance, and their families, have endured the torture, poverty, and irremediable dishonor. They may be meek and hallowed men, willing to endure ; and as for my wife — what was she to you? Ye cannot be greatly disturbed that she is in her grave. No, ye are quiet, calm, prudent persons ; it would be a most indiscreet thing of you, you who have suffered no wrongs yourselves, to stir on her account.

" In truth, friends, Mr. Renwick is quite right. This feeling of indignation against our oppressors is a most imprudent thing. If we desire to enjoy our own contempt, to deserve the derision of men, and to merit the abhorrence of Heaven, let us yield ourselves to all that Charles Stuart and his sect require. We can do nothing better, nothing so meritorious, — nothing by which we can so reasonably hope for punishment here and condemnation hereafter. But if there is one man at this meeting, — I am speaking not of shapes and forms, but of feelings, — if there is one here that feels as men were wont to feel, he will draw his sword, and say with me, Woe to the house of Stuart! woe to the o ressors!""

'Impassioned' pieces, such as the last of the example above and the following, should have 'very loud force,' 'very long slides,' 'very abrupt stress.' Time accelerating as the passion cumulates, from 'moderate' to 'faster,' with 'very long quantity' on the emphatic words, 'middle and higher pitch' and 'quality' (where the passion is not malignant), only slightly 'aspirated.'

Impassioned example.

" 'My castles are my king's alone,
  From turret to foundation stone;
  The hand of Douglas is his own,
  And never shall in friendly grasp
  The hand of such as Marmion clasp!'
  Burned Marmion's swarthy cheek like **fire**,
  And shook his very frame for ire,
  And 'This to me!' he said;
  'An't were not for thy hoary beard,
  Such hand as Marmion's had not spared
  To cleave the Douglas' head!
  And, Douglas, more I tell thee here
  E'en in thy pitch of pride,
  Here, in thy hold, thy vassals near,
  I tell thee, thou'rt defied!
  And if thou saidst I am not peer
  To any lord in Scotland here,
  Lowland or Highland, far or near,
  Lord Angus, thou hast lied!'
  On the earl's cheek the flush of rage
  O'ercame the ashen hue of age;
  Fierce he broke forth: 'And dar'st thou, **then,**
  To beard the lion in his den,
  The Douglas in his hall?
  And hop'st thou hence unscathed to go?
  No! by Saint Bride of Bothwell, no!
  Up drawbridge, groom! What, warder, **ho!**
  Let the portcullis fall!' "

POETIC READING.

To read poetry well we must study, —.

I. The ideas, — the sense and spirit.

II. The metre, — the kind and number of "feet" in the respective lines.

III. The proper blending of the sense and the measure, — the rhythm of the verse.

The first and most important part — the right reading of the sense and spirit — we have anticipated in our general instructions.

MEASURE AND METRE.

The agreeable variety of accented and unaccented syllables, of longer and shorter quantities, in our English speech, is rendered more pleasing to the ear in *English verse* by being arranged in some regular *proportion* and *order* and *recurrence*.

In the regular proportion of *one accented* to *one unaccented* syllable we have, as a unit of measure, the dissyllabic foot, called an *iambus* or a *trochee*, according as it is arranged in the one or the other of two regular orders.

FIRST ORDER (*iambic*).

"Must wé | but blúsh ? | our fá | thers bléd."

SECOND ORDER (*trochaic*).

"Líves of | greát men | áll re | mínd us."

In the regular proportion of *one accented* to *two unaccented* syllables we have, as a unit of measure, the trisyllabic foot, called an *anapest*, or a *dactyl*, according as it is arranged in the one or the other of two regular orders.

FIRST ORDER (*anapestic*).

"'Tis the clíme | of the éast, | 'tis the lánd | of the sún."

SECOND ORDER (*dactylic*).

"Stréw the fair | gárlands where | slúmber the | déad."

The *foot* is easily determined by the number and order of the unaccented syllables.

The *metre* is determined by the number of feet in the respective lines ; as "five-foot," "four-foot," "two-foot," and "four-foot" in the order given in the lines below, in "iambic measure."

"There wás | a tíme | when méad | ow, gróve, | and stréam, .
The éarth | and év | ery cóm | mon síght,
To mé | did seém
Appár | elled ín | celés | tial líght." ·

PROSAIC READING AND "SING-SONG."

The two great faults in the reading of poetry are, *prosaic* reading, which aims to give the meaning only, with no regard for the music of verse, and *scanning,* or "sing-song," which chops the lines into their metric parts, and emphasizes each foot separately, with a monotonous movement, accent, and pause, which destroy both the sense and the melody.

To remedy the first fault, which turns poetry into prose, the *measure* must be made the prominent study for a while. Musical lines, in which the thoughts and words flow smoothly into, and fill the metre, must be often read, until the ear and taste learn to appreciate their metric charm.

To remedy the fault of "sing-song," which overmarks the metre, the *sense* must be especially emphasized for a time, and the words grouped to give the meaning rather than the metre.

But to remedy both of these extremes, the *rhythm,* which harmonizes the sensè and the measure, must be mastered.

RHYTHM.

The foot and metre of verse may be shown by merely scanning it, but the rhythm can be heard only as the flowing whole is read.

Rhythm is the opposite of scanning. Scanning is the analysis or cutting up of the lines into their separate feet. Rhythm is the synthesis, or flowing together of the separate feet into such *larger groups,* and with such varying accent and measured time, as give both the sense and melody of verse.

A little scanning is introduced here partly to show *what not to do* in reading, and partly to present more clearly, by contrast, the nature and use of rhythm.

RHYTHMIC GROUPING, ACCENT, AND PAUSES.

"The mél | anchól | y dáys | are cóme, | the sád | dest óf |
   the yéar,
Of wáiling wínds, and náked woóds, and méadows brówn and
   sére."

In scanning this first line of "seven-foot" metre in the usual way, it is divided into *seven* groups, with seven uniform accents and pauses.

In the rhythmic reading, which accords with the sense, these seven "feet" flow naturally into only *two* groups.

And the seven monotonous accents also are changed to four significant ones which give the meaning, and three unemphatic ones merely metric, so light as not to mar the sense or flow, and yet distinct enough to preserve the metre ; as thus : —

"The *mel*ancholy *days* are come, —
   The *sad*dest of the *year*."

The seven feet of the second line flow into *three* groups. Note how the sense so fills the measure in this line that the emphatic and metric accents agree in number.

"Of wailing winds — and naked woods —
   And meadows brown and sere."

Observe, also, that the "seven-foot" metre of the lines just quoted may as well be written and read as they are here grouped, in the "common metre" of alternate "four-foot" and "three-foot" lines.

This shows that mere metre has less to do with natural reading than rhythmic grouping. The lines in Shakespeare are nearly all of *one measure* and *metre*, and would sound much *alike* in *scanning*. Yet what infinite *variety* of grouping and expression they demand in their perfect reading!

TIME AS MOVEMENT AND QUANTITY.

In lines like the last the feet are numbered by the accents, and so they are in trisyllabic measure.

"For the móon never béams without brínging me dréams
     Of the beaútiful Ánnabel Lée,
And the stars never rise but I feel the bright eyes
     Of my beautiful Annabel Lee."

The number of accents is the same in these lines; but the movement and time mark the difference in the rhythm and measure. Time is the chief element in the measurement of verse.

The standard time, as fast or slow, varies, as in prose, with the spirit of the poem; but the relative time in verse is metric, —that is to say, the several feet which flow together in a given logical group should have an equal share of the time given to that group. One whole group may be joyous, and the next group may be sad, and so the general time change suddenly from fast to slow: but the associated feet may and should be measured with equable time, if the poet's chosen words allow of it; and if they do not allow of this, then the verse is not musical, and the sense alone should be read.

THE FINAL AND CÆSURAL PAUSES.

Pauses in verse, as in prose, are used to separate the ideas. The lines are usually separated from each other by a pause demanded by the sense. But when the sense would group the last of one line with the first of the next line, the sense and rhythm both forbid any final pause. The voice should linger on the final foot long enough to give its *full metric quantity*, but no break is allowable.

"And dark as winter — was *the flow*
     Of Iser, rolling rapidly."

"All is finished! and at length
     Has come the bridal day
     Of beauty and of strength."

> " Ready *to be*
> The bride of the gray old sea."

In the last example the *quantity* of the foot *"to be"* is length-ened to fill the metric time, and to mark the rhyme with *" sea."*

In Bryant's " Forest Hymn," in " five-foot " iambic verse, several consecutive lines flow on with no *final* pause.

> " For his simple heart
> Might not resist the sacred influences,
> Which from the stilly twilight of the place,
> And from the gray old trunks that high in heaven
> Mingled their mossy boughs, and from the sound
> Of the invisible breath that swayed at once
> All their green tops, stole over him and bowed
> His spirit with the thought of boundless power
> And inaccessible majesty.   Ah, why
> Should we, in the world's riper years, neglect
> God's ancient sanctuaries, and adore
> Only among the crowd, and under roofs
> That our frail hands have raised ? "

THE CÆSURAL PAUSE.

The " cæsura " is a peculiar pause of the sense in the line which breaks a *foot*, one part of which foot flows with the group before the pause, and the other part of the same foot flows with the group after the pause.

This cæsura does not affect the rhythm or reading of verse any more than other pauses.   It affects the scanning merely. This cæsural foot is often made of two *short* and *unaccented* syllables, and is then marked by time only.

The time of the natural pauses of emphasis, and pauses which separate the ideas, is counted in reading the lines only so far as it is needed to equalize the measure.   When thus needed, the pause affects the measure like a *rest* in *music.*

> " When Frée | dom — from | her móun | tain heíght
>   Unfúrled | her stánd | ard — to | the air,
>   She tóre the ázure róbe of níght,
>   And sét the stárs of glóry thére ! "

In the second foot of the first, and in the third foot of the second line occurs the *cæsural* foot, unaccented. In reading these lines, a *rest* equivalent to a *short* syllable is needed in the cæsural feet.

> " When Frēe | dŏm ‿ frŏm | hĕr mōun | tăin heīght
>   Unfūrled | hĕr stānd | ărd ‿ tŏ | thĕ aīr."

The poet in this example has utilized the short pause, making it an essential part of the measure, and the lines *musical*. In the other lines the syllables alone fill the measure.

Sometimes the *pause* of *emphasis* is likewise used as a proportional part of the measure of a line.

> "*Hárk !* | 'tis the voíce | of the móun | tain,
>   .And it spéaks | to our heárt | in its príde,
>   And it tells | of the bear | ing of he | roes
>   Who com | passed its sum | mits and died."

Observe the use of the emphatic *monosyllabic foot* "*hark,*" and of the *dissyllabic foot* at the beginning of the last line "*who com.*" Such feet are allowed, by poetic usage, when they can take the *same time* as the regular feet have.

It is not claimed that all lines can be thus exactly measured. The pause is often *extra* time and arbitrary in the verse.

When the regular rhythm will give the sense it should be assumed to be the poet's reading. In the lines

> " Líves of gréat men áll remínd us
>   Wé can máke our líves sublíme,"

the trochaic reading must be preferred, which gives the sense by a strong accent on " *we,*" and preserves the rhythm in harmony with the other lines.

" We can make *our* lives sublime " gives the sense only.

An agreeable variety in the *flow* of verse is often introduced into dissyllabic measure by the use of a foot of three
syllables.

> " And whát | is so ráre | as a dáy | in Júne ?
> Thén if | éver | come pér | fect dáys ;
> Then Heáven | tríes the earth | if it bé | in túne,
> And ó | ver it sóft | ly her wárm | ear láys."

The measure of time is the same in the first line as if written
thus : " And what | so rare | as days | in June."
Yet the added syllables give a pleasing rhythmic variety,
which makes half the charm of the verse. Note, also, that the
second line begins with trochaic feet and ends with iambic ;
thus still further varying the rhythmic beauty. And in the
third line the accents of the first two feet come together. If
read rapidly this would break the melody roughly on the ear.
But the natural pause on the emphatic word "Heaven" gives
time to change the rhythm without offence.

Sometimes these exceptional " feet " are used to give variety
to the verse and often to accommodate the sense.
The trisyllabic measure often begins or ends with a foot of
two syllables and sometimes of *one* long syllable.

> " Ōh, yoúng | Lochinvár | is come oút | from the Wést ! "

> " Dēar Fá | ther, take cáre | of thy chíl | dren, the bóys."

The unaccented syllable in the first foot is " long," and equals
in metric time the two unaccented syllables in the standard foot.

> " Déar to each | heárt are the | námes of the | bráve ;
> Résting in | glóry, how | swéetly they | sléep !
> Déw-drops at | évening fall | sóft on each | gráve,
> Kíndred and | stróngers bend | fóndly to | wéep."

These dactylic lines end with a foot of *one* accented syllable,
which, being at the end of the line and emphatic, can be agreeably prolonged to fill the standard time.

Sometimes the emphasis of the sense overmasters the **regular** metric accent.

"Has there án | y old fél | low got míxed | with the bóys?"

would be the regular accentuation; yet the word "*old*" is the most emphatic syllable in the line, being in contrast to "*boys*," and must therefore take the strong accent of sense, thus, —

"Has there án | y *óld* fel | low got míxed | with the bóys?"

The change does not affect the time of the measure, only the rhythm, by putting the accent on the middle syllable in the second foot.

Iambic lines very often begin with a trochaic foot.

"Úp from | the méad | ow rích | with córn,
Cléar in | the cóol | Septém | ber mórn."

When consecutive trisyllabic words occur in an iambic or trochaic line, they give in reading the rhythmic variety of the other measure.

"Beaúti | ful Év | elyn Hópe | is déad."

This line may be scanned in several ways, yet in natural reading it takes this form best, —

"Beaútiful | Évelyn | Hópe — | is déad,"

with two "dactyls," one "monosyllabic" foot, and one iambic. This is the natural grouping of the words and sense, and better preserves the music of the verse.

Finally, GROUP the words so as best to give the SENSE. VARY THE ACCENT in force and place to give the sense. Suit the general time to the general spirit of each group. But let the feet associated in any given group be read with the SAME relative EQUABLE TIME, as far as the poet's words will allow.

In a word, read the SENSE ALWAYS, read the measure when you can.

CPSIA information can be obtained
at www.ICGtesting.com
Printed in the USA
BVHW051846051118
532208BV00023B/4362/P

9 780483 191853